'If all be true that I do think
There are five reasons we should drink
Good wine . . . a friend . . . or being dry—
Or lest we should be by and by
Or any other reason why . . .'

Reasons for Drinking, Dean Aldrich
(1647–1710)

THE LONDON

BOOK OF

—JENNIE REEKIE—

Ebury Press
LONDON

First published by Ebury Press
an imprint of the Random Century Group
Random Century House
20 Vauxhall Bridge Road London SW1V 2SA

**British Library Cataloguing in
Publication Data**
Reekie, Jennie
  The London Ritz book of drinks.
  1. Drinks—Recipes
  I. Title
  641.87
  ISBN 0-85223-814-2

Filmset by
Advanced Filmsetters (Glasgow) Ltd
Printed in Great Britain
at the University Press, Cambridge

Acknowledgements
The author would like to thank Terry Holmes,
Bob Burton, Drago Marinov and
Michael Simms of The Ritz Hotel, London,
and Roger Ellis of Ritz Products for their help.

The publishers would like to thank the
following for permission to reprint copyright
material:

Page 61 reprinted by permission of
Hutchinson Ltd from *Carry on Jeeves* by
P. G. Wodehouse

Pages 8, 9, 58 reprinted by permission of
Aurum Press from *The London Ritz: A Social
and Architectural History* by Hugh
Montgomery-Massingberd and David Watkin

As well as giving recipes for drinks and
canapés served at The Ritz Hotel, London, this
book includes many additional ideas. The
hotel does not serve all the drinks and canapés
for which recipes are given here.

Text: Jennie Reekie
Editors: Geri Gibbons, Carol McGlynn
Illustrators: Mei Lim, Dennis and
Sheila Curran

A Note on Measures
The standard drinks measure in Britain is $\frac{1}{6}$ gill
(a gill being an old-fashioned term for $\frac{1}{4}$ pint),
i.e. 0.83 fl oz or 25 ml. In this book measures
have been rounded up to 30 ml/1 fl oz, but if
you have a standard measure this can be used
instead. Equally, 1 fl oz is equal to
2 tablespoons and $\frac{1}{4}$ fl oz is equal to
$1\frac{1}{2}$ teaspoons.

Contents

'There are two reasons for drinking; one is, when you are thirsty, to cure it; the other, when you are not thirsty, to prevent it.'

Thomas Love Peacock (1785–1866)

The Bar at the Ritz

Sitting and enjoying a quiet drink at the Ritz Bar is one of life's unique experiences. The surroundings retain all the sumptuous elegance of a bygone era and it requires little effort to imagine an Edwardian beauty wafting past, possibly Edward VII's mistress Alice Keppel, a regular patron of the hotel, or even Anna Pavlova, who danced here in May 1912.

The present bar is a voyeur's paradise, situated as it is in the Long Gallery between the Main Hall and the Palm Court so that hotel guests, or people entering the hotel from Arlington Street, have to walk through on their way to the dining room.

Sitting on one of the gilded Louis XVI chairs, you can idly watch not only the beautifully dressed men and women who sit down for a drink, but also those who simply pass by.

In the Palm Court, which in the afternoons is reserved exclusively for tea, drinks are served prior to lunch as well as pre- and post-dinner. The Palm Court, or Winter Garden as it is also known, is without doubt one of the most beautiful rooms in London. Designed by César Ritz, it has steps leading up to it 'so that ladies entering...or leaving may do so dramatically,' according to his widow. Panelled mirrors at the back flank a fountain, at the centre of which is the celebrated 'nymph', and the whole room is swathed in a pale, soft light emanating from the frosted glass ceiling and the chandeliers.

The Bar is presided over by Bob Burton who, during his ten-year tenure, has devised over 200 different cocktails. Some are named after the rich or famous who have patronized his Bar, while others mark special occasions or may just be ideas he has dreamed up in one of his few quiet moments. Provided he is not too busy, he will even create a cocktail especially for you.

As most cocktails contain some form of fruit liqueur, he first asks you for your favourite fruit, so that he can select a fruit base you will enjoy, and then for your favourite spirit. Armed with this information, he sets to work mixing in

A PUBLIC STAGE

'. . . (in 1934) the Duke of Kent married Princess Marina of Greece and the Ritz erected scaffolding in the garden for the occasion. Sir Cecil Beaton recalled, shortly before he died, that the pianist Edyth Baker was greatly upset by being what she regarded as jilted by Prince George; instead of crying alone in her room Miss Baker chose to make a public display of her unhappiness, tedious through repetition, in the Rivoli Bar at the Ritz.'

The London Ritz,
Hugh Montgomery-Massingberd and
David Watkin

a small glass to obtain the correct proportions of all the different ingredients—tasting as he goes. Once he has established the basic 'recipe', into the cocktail shaker go the various dashes of this and that, he gives a quick shake and behold—your very own cocktail. The work of a wizard!

Despite its air of permanence, the Long Gallery is not the original bar, for it was previously the hotel lounge. There used to be both a bar in the basement, and the Rivoli Bar at the front of the hotel which opened on to Piccadilly, now a row of exclusive shops. The downstairs bar was always the more popular and after the war was frequented by the likes of Evelyn Waugh, Graham Greene, Lady Diana Cooper, and even Tallulah Bankhead when she performed a cabaret season at the Café de Paris. Writing in the late 1950s the journalist Ian Dunlop observed that the 'Rivoli Bar, upstairs, was a place where hardly anybody knew you very much, and you could go and have a drink with the person you shouldn't be having a drink with. If you wanted to see people whom you knew, you went downstairs to the basement bar where Laurie held his court and everybody knew everybody.'

Laurie was Laurie Ross who for many years ran the downstairs bar which became affectionately known as 'Laurie's Bar'. Following his death in 1985 Peregrine Worsthorne wrote a touching obituary in the *Daily Telegraph*.

> ... Laurie saw life through rose-coloured spectacles but that was what made him such a superb barman. All his old clients were treated in a manner appropriate to the status of 'a gentleman of the old school'.
>
> He flattered us outrageously and cosseted our egos—just as important a quality in a barman as being able to mix a good dry martini.
>
> I suppose he was a bit of an actor. He cannot really always have been so pleased to see one as he seemed. But so convincing was his performance that while at his bar and under his aegis, one felt oneself to be the most elegant, important, amusing person in town.
>
> No wonder we all loved Laurie and returned to the Ritz bar, decade after decade, like homing pigeons.

The barman is the central pivot of any bar and today Bob Burton carries on the traditions of his predecessors. Drinking, like eating, should be a pleasurable activity carried out at leisure,

'He who goes to bed, and goes to bed sober,
Falls as the leaves do and dies in October;
But he who goes to bed, and goes to bed
  mellow
Lives as he ought to do, and dies an honest
  fellow.'

Anon

in surroundings conducive to relaxation and enjoyment. The Bar at the Ritz provides all these things: comfort, service and an ambiance which is to be found in no other hotel in a capital city.

In a world in which there is a depressing amount of uniformity—indeed, it is the proud boast of some hotel chains that once you have entered the portals of their establishment you could be anywhere on the globe—the Ritz has retained its individuality, and the Bar *still* has its regular customers.

'There is absolutely no scientific proof of a trustworthy kind that moderate consumption of sound alcoholic liquor does a healthy body any harm at all; whilst on the other hand there is unbroken testimony of all history that alcoholic liquors have been used by the strongest, wisest, handsomest, and in every way best, races of all time.'

Notes on a Cellar Book 1920,
George Saintsbury

The Ritz Cellar

Were César Ritz himself to walk into the Ritz cellars today he would feel entirely at home, for they have changed little since the hotel opened in 1906. The chief difference, much to the chagrin of the present cellar master, Drago Marinov, is that they are now smaller, for they used to extend right under the pavement, an area now used by the shops which have the Piccadilly frontage.

A degree in chemical engineering from Bucharest University seems an unusual qualification for this prestigious position, but Drago appears oblivious of its incongruity and what shines through is his love for, and knowledge of, wines. When he picks up a dusty bottle of Château Petrus 1970 (value £550), he is not being careful merely because it is an expensive object—he handles it like a baby and looks at it in reverence, caring for it just as though it were one of his children.

At one time the cellar master, together with the head sommelier, would travel to France to buy their wines 'en primeur' direct from the vineyards, but with such fine quality wines now coming from all over the world, this practice ceased a few years ago. Now, four or five times a year they hold blind wine tastings, which are attended by Drago and his assistant, Michael Simms, the head sommelier, and his assistant, and any other staff who wish to attend. At these tastings up to twelve different suppliers will submit samples of their wines and the assembled company choose the wines they think are most suited to a particular price range for the wine list.

If it is a wine from the lower end of the price range, the Ritz will take an option on it and, apart from the necessary stock, the majority will be retained by the shipper. Should it be a fine wine, it will quickly be found a place in the cellar, for Drago likes to keep an eye on his superior products and ensure that they are kept at an even temperature of 12° Celsius (54–56° Fahrenheit).

Below Stairs...

The cellar itself is on two levels, with the lower level reserved for Champagnes and white wines. It is in the area of white wines in particular that the Ritz has moved with the times and, in addition to the French wines one would expect to find, there are wines from California, Italy, Australia, Cyprus, Spain, South Africa and Hungary, as well as English wines from the vineyards of Lamberhurst, Barton Manor and Adgestone. It is not merely among the red wines where jewels are to be found; the cellar also boasts the king of Sauternes, a Château d'Yquem 1976—reputed to be the finest accompaniment to *foie gras*. If indulging in this particular luxury, £250 seems little to pay for the wine to go with it!

A flight of rickety stairs leads to the reds, where French wines predominate (although there are others, including a couple from Drago's native Bulgaria). Many of the red wines are bought at least three or four years before they are fit for drinking, to be certain of availability and in advance of their price becoming exorbitant. They paid only £8.70 for the Château Petrus in 1976, for example—a canny investment. For the few who can afford to drink them, Drago points out, these expensive wines are a 'good buy', for no matter what bottle you are consuming in the restaurant you have to pay excise duty, VAT, and service charges, which makes them seem almost a bargain!

There are still a few remaining bottles of a Château Latour 1949, which needs re-corking every twenty years or so. Recently the head cellarer of Château Latour made the journey from France to perform the ceremony and, having been informed of the number of bottles the Ritz had in stock, came with one cork too few, on the pretext that it was quite *essential* he checked the wine was still in mint condition!

Once the wines leave the cellar, they come into the care of Michael Simms. A few bottles of each of the 360-odd wines on the list are kept

> 'It ought to give pause to the most fanatical teetotaller that the only humans worth saving in the Flood were a family of vintners.'
>
> Now I Lay Me Down To Eat,
> Dr Bernard Rudofsky

in the dispense bar in the kitchen so that they are always at the correct temperature for serving. Michael is passionate about his subject and spends much of his spare time educating himself, and his palate, still further. Not exactly unpleasurable work as it involves plenty of eating and drinking which he clearly enjoys! He has won numerous competitions and represented Great Britain at the European Sommelier Championships.

Always delighted when those dining in the restaurant seek his advice on the wine to accompany their meal, his only frustration is when, having given his view—possibly at some length—the customer *then* announces that he never drinks red wine, for example, or dislikes whites from Alsace; information that would have been helpful if given in advance. He is also extremely patient when rung in the late afternoon by a panic-stricken host or hostess demanding to know what wines to serve at that evening's dinner party!

César Ritz

Serving Wine

Serving wine at the correct temperature is as important as the original choice of wine, for a bottle of fine wine can be ruined if drunk too warm or too cold, while even a mediocre bottle will taste considerably better if consumed at the right temperature.

Red Bordeaux, wines from the Rhône and Italian wines (and their counterparts from other countries) should be opened about one hour before serving and should be drunk at the same temperature as the environment in which they are being consumed. Red Burgundies and their equivalents should not be opened beforehand and are served slightly cooler, around 60–65° Fahrenheit.

White wines should be served chilled and the most satisfactory way to do this is in a bucket of ice for at least twenty minutes before serving. The cork should be removed from the bottle prior to plunging it into the ice, and then replaced loosely.

Pass the Port

The British liking for port dates from around 1703, when the Duke of Marlborough was engaged in battle with Louis XIV of France. To discourage trade with the enemy, Queen Anne increased the duty on French wines to £55 a tun and at the same time signed a treaty with Portugal which decreed that a mere £7 per tun was payable on their wines—hence these few lines from Jonathan Swift.

> Be sometimes to your country true.
> Have once the public good in view.
> Bravely despise Champagne at Court,
> And choose to dine at home with Port.

Throughout the eighteenth century, right up until 1815, French wines continued to command exorbitant prices owing to duties, wars and revolutions. In 1762 at the Pleasure Gardens in Vauxhall a bottle of port cost 2 shillings, while a bottle of Champagne was four times the price. Thus port became established as the most popular wine in Britain, causing a contemporary writer to comment, 'He is believed to have liked port, but to have said of claret, that it would be port if it could.'

By far the great majority of the port drunk was of the non-vintage variety consumed in public houses and this remained the case until the mid-1930s, when 80 percent of the port shipped to Britain was drunk as 'port and lemon'. However, the advent of the cocktail in the 1920s had already started to drastically reduce the quantity of port consumed each year.

It is vintage port, though, that is the connoisseur's drink. Beloved by colonels in their

THE HOST'S TASTE

The practice of pouring a small quantity of wine into the host's glass for him to taste is thought to have originated on the Continent before the widespread use of corks for stoppering bottles. Most wine was stored in casks, but would be kept in bottles for periods of up to a couple of months. The bottles were fragile, unlike their modern counterparts, and so had to be kept upright and the easiest way to prevent oxidization of the wine was to pour in a thin layer of olive oil, which effectively sealed it.

Before the wine was served, the oil would be carefully poured away, but there was always the chance that a few drops might remain on the surface of the wine. By serving himself first, with a small quantity, the master of the house could then be certain that it was only *his* wine, and not that of his guests, which might be tainted. As practised today, the custom is a way of ascertaining that the wine is in good condition and is indeed what the customer ordered.

clubs, or by men at dinner, once the ladies had retired from the room, it is now considered acceptable for the ladies to share this ambrosial drink—provided they remember to pass the decanter to the left! Various reasons are given for the origin of this time-honoured custom;

two of the most popular being that it is connected with the Royal Navy, where port means left, or that it follows the natural path of the sun, i.e. clockwise.

Vintage port, more than any other wine, needs plenty of time to mature. The Ritz like to buy twenty-five years in advance so, for those lucky enough to enjoy a bottle of port there in the year 2000, on offer will be bottles from the 1977 vintage (considered to be an excellent year, possibly the best since '27) and the 1983 vintage. Today's customers can still sip a Taylor's '27 or '35 if their wallets are fat enough, but if not there are plenty of less exalted vintages on the list at more reasonable prices.

V.S.O.P.

The letters V.S.O.P. on a bottle of Cognac stand for Very Special Old Pale, indicating just how long the trade with Britain has lasted and how important the British have always been as customers.

randy

Claret is the liquor for boys; port for men; but he who aspires to be a hero must drink brandy.

Samuel Johnson at dinner with
Sir Joshua Reynolds (*Boswell's Life*, 1779)

Many countries produce brandy. Indeed the British, past masters at the art of distilling gin and whisky, found much of the wine that entered the country quite undrinkable and their only recourse was to distil it. For centuries much of this coarse spirit, together with cheap distillations from France, was drunk with water, in the same way as Scotch. It may well have been what Dorothy Wordsworth, the poet's sister, had been imbibing on a picnic with her brother and Coleridge when she wrote 'I drank a little brandy and water, and was in heaven!' for it would have been highly alcoholic.

These young spirits would have born no relation to the well-developed, mature flavour of what are now considered to be the two finest brandies, Cognac and Armagnac, both from France. The only people likely to disagree with that statement are the Spanish, who also produce some excellent brandies.

As with some other superb examples of food and drink, the birth of Cognac was a happy accident rather than design. Around 1630 a number of factors, including the lack of quality in their wines, forced the wine producers in an area 100 miles north of Bordeaux to stop selling their wines straight and to distil them, and they found a ready market for the product in England. However, the War of the Spanish Succession between 1701 and 1713 caused a temporary cessation in trade and in order to preserve the brandy they were forced to store it in oak casks for several years. In so doing, they discovered they had produced an altogether smoother, fuller-flavoured drink.

Armagnac has always been a more popular brandy in its native France than in England, but has recently found favour here and indeed become almost a cult. For any devotee of Armagnac a pilgrimage to the Ritz is almost essential, for they can serve you a glass of 1893 Michel Faure, or—if funds will not stretch to that at £40 a glass—a 1904 costs a mere £28!

> 'Within the cellar's cool domain
> I exercise my sway, sir;
> Of Burgundy the Soverain
> And county of Tokay, sir;
> My rubies stir in every flask
> Should I but set it clinking;
> Come tapster, broach your noblest cask
> For my drinking, drinking, drinking.'
>
> Drinking Song, Carl Müchler

Drinking Vessels

Glass-making is thought to have been discovered in Mesopotamia around 2000 BC, one thousand years before the Egyptians perfected the art of moulding and, far more importantly, the Syrians that of blowing glass to make vessels. Glass was originally used by the Egyptians solely for glazing jewellery and ceramic objects.

In essence, glass-making is a very simple technique, requiring only heat to fuse silica, in the form of sand or quartz, with soda or potash. That it can produce such exquisitely delicate objects has long been a source of amazement. As one James Howell re-

marked in the seventeenth century, '... a rare kind of knowledge and chemistry to transmit dust and sand (for they are the only main ingredients) to such a diaphanous, pellucid, dainty body as you see a Crystal-Glass is ....'

The size of the Roman Empire resulted in the skills of glass-blowing spreading far and wide, not only around the Middle East but also throughout Northern Europe. Even though few examples remain from Roman times, it is known that these were not crude vessels, but beautiful pieces, requiring a considerable amount of intricate work. Following the fall of Rome, it was not until about the eleventh century that there was a renaissance of the art, but by the fifteenth century Venice had established itself as the centre for glass-making. At the time of his death in 1547 Henry VIII had amassed an extensive collection of Venetian glass. It was from Venice that a number of craftsmen came to Britain during the sixteenth century—indeed it is possible that some of Henry's 'Venetian glass' was in fact made in Britain. The 'glasshouses' were generally established in densely wooded areas, so that there was plenty of fuel readily available to fire the furnaces. Such was the destruction of the forests, however, that in 1615 a law was passed forbidding wood to be used in glass furnaces, so the glassmakers had to move to areas where coal was plentiful.

Georgian Glass

Among antique buffs, glasses made between 1685 and 1850 are considered to be the finest collectors' pieces. Little remains of earlier glass for after a few years it began to decompose, causing a semi-opaque effect known as 'crizzling'. By the end of the seventeenth century this problem had been overcome by adding minute quantities of lead to the glass, which not only prevented crizzling but produced a clearer glass. The mid-eighteenth century also saw the introduction of new furnaces which heated the glass to a much higher temperature, enabling the glass-blowers to produce glass of a brilliance far superior to anything that had been seen before.

Many of the glasses of this period are beautifully engraved or cut, and some have remarkable stems, with air twists or mixed-colour twists of enamel which makes them quite exceptional. There was logic behind this superb craftsmanship for, owing to the heavy tax on glass by weight, which was not repealed until 1845, it was more profitable to make lightweight glasses, and decorate them, than to make heavier, plain glasses. Almost all the glasses were considerably smaller than they are now, i.e. the wine glasses were only 50–75 ml/2–3 fl oz (¼–⅜ cup) as against 150–200 ml/5–8 fl oz (⅝–1 cup) today. Another effect of the tax was that a number of glass-makers went to live in Ireland in order to escape it, and founded a highly successful glass industry there.

Drinks for Glasses, Glasses for Drinks

As early as 1670 one John Green, a member of the Glass Sellers Company, stipulated when buying glass from Venice that he must have specific glasses for sack, claret, beer, Rhenish, brandy and French wine. He sent illustrations with his order, showing tumblers for beer, claret and sack, rounded funnel bowls on short stems for French wine, and hollow-stemmed glasses for the sweeter German Rhenish, as it was known. In order to boost sales throughout the eighteenth century, glass-sellers promoted the notion that certain glasses were required for particular drinks. The idea quickly caught on amongst society hostesses, always keen to outdo each other, with fashions in the shape of drinking glasses coming and going.

After the end of the Napoleonic Wars, when Champagne was being drunk again, it was initially served in flute glasses. In the late 1820s a hemispherical bowl became fashionable, which Disraeli described in 1832 as a 'saucer of ground glass mounted upon a pedestal of cut glass', but by 1858 the tulip glass had gained vogue for drinking Champagne.

Currently there are a plethora of different shapes and sizes of drinking glasses to choose from, but there are no hard and fast rules which have to be slavishly followed. In some cases there are reasons why a drink is served in a particular glass, for example so that one can better appreciate the bouquet or colour, but it is rarely essential. One thing is usually true though—the better the quality of the glass, the better the drink tastes!

Wine glasses
These come in all shapes and sizes, but are always stemmed. Traditionally white wine glasses are smaller and have longer stems than those used for red wine, which should have a well-rounded bowl to allow the wine to breathe.

Champagne flute
A tall, fluted glass with a stem, used for Champagne or other sparkling wine and for Champagne-based cocktails.

Tulip glass
A tall, tulip-shaped glass used in the same way as the Champagne glass.

Copita
A small, tulip-shaped glass which is especially good for sherry so that its flavour and aroma can be fully appreciated; it is also used for white wines.

Liqueur glass
A small, stemmed glass used for serving liqueurs and port.

Brandy balloon
A stemmed glass with a wide base and narrow rim designed to trap the fragrance of the brandy so that both bouquet and flavour can be enjoyed.

Sour glass
A stemmed glass, similar to a white wine glass, which holds approx 180 ml/6 fl oz/¾ cup.

Ballon glass
Basically a wine glass, but a large one which can be used for cocktails and even lagers. Holds approx 300 ml/10 fl oz/1¼ cups.

Large goblet
These vary considerably in size and shape but usually have a wide rim, so are suitable for exotic cocktails which are served with plenty of decoration.

Cocktail or martini glass
A wide-rimmed glass with a tall stem, used for martinis and other cocktails. Holds approx 120 ml/4 fl oz/½ cup.

Old-fashioned or whisky tumbler
A short tumbler with straight or sloping sides in which cocktails on the rocks are served, as well as whisky and water or soda. Holds approx 180 ml/6 fl oz/¾ cup.

Highball or tall glass
A tall, straight-sided glass used for long drinks, such as gin and tonic. Holds approx 250 ml/8 fl oz/1 cup.

Collins
Bigger version of the highball. Holds approx 300 ml/10 fl oz/1¼ cups.

'Some men are like musical glasses—to produce their finest tones you must keep them wet.'
Table Talk, T Coleridge

FROSTING GLASSES

Frosting the rim of a glass not only looks attractive but also enhances the flavour of a drink and, in some cases, such as the salt frosting on a Margarita, is an essential part of the recipe.

Sugar frosting *Dip the rim of the glass into lemon juice or lightly beaten egg white to a depth of about 0.75 cm/¼ inch and then dip into caster sugar or fine brown sugar. To add colour to a fruit-based cocktail, white sugar can be coloured with a little food colouring.*

Salt frosting *Dip the rim of the glass into lime juice and then into fine salt. Celery salt can also be used and adds to the flavour of tomato-based drinks, such as a Bloody Mary.*

Coconut *Desiccated coconut makes an interesting frosting for fruit cocktails, especially if they contain a coconut-based liqueur. Dip the rim of the glass in lightly beaten egg white and then in finely grated desiccated coconut.*

Coffee and chocolate *Coffee or chocolate-based liqueur drinks can be served frosted with the relevant ingredient. Dip the glass into lightly beaten egg white and then into either instant coffee powder or drinking chocolate.*

Flagons and Tankards

St George he was for England,
And, before he killed the dragon,
He drank a pint of English ale
Out of an English flagon.

G K Chesterton

Originally sacramental vessels used for the communion wine, flagons were the forerunners of tankards. Made out of silver, pewter, stoneware or porcelain, their size made them convenient receptacles for drinking beer and cider once they had been consigned to secular use. By the Middle Ages, the words flagon and tankard had become virtually interchangeable.

Many tankards were made of pewter or earthenware, with pewter or silver lids as described by a French priest, Etienne Perlin, who visited England in 1558. 'They [the English] consume great quantities of beer, double and single, and drink it, not out of glasses, but from earthenware pots with handles and covers of silver, even in houses of persons of medium wealth, and as for the poor, the covers of their pots are only of pewter, and in some villages their beer pots are made of wood.'

Some tankards of the period, however, were

a great deal more ornate, for when Queen Elizabeth I went on one of her many tours around the country, Lady Cobham presented her with 'oone tankerede of allablaster garnished with silver and guilt'.

As English ale then bore no resemblance to today's gaseous preparations, up until the nineteenth century all tankards had lids to them, which were opened by a thumbpiece on the

'Go fetch to me a pint o' wine,
    An' fill it in a silver tassie;
That I may drink before I go
    A service to my bonnie lassie.'

Farewell, Robert Burns

handle. Yards of ale were popular after the seventeenth century and in 1685 John Evelyn recorded drinking the King's health in a 'flint glass of a yard long'.

IRISH COFFEE

*'Cream, rich as an Irish brogue
Coffee, strong as a friendly hand,
Sugar, sweet as the tongue of a rogue
Whiskey, smooth as the wit of the land.'*

Anon

Irish, or Gaelic coffee as it is also known, is unusual in that it is a hot coffee drink which by tradition is served in a wine glass, rather than a cup or a mug. To prevent the glass from cracking and also to keep the drink hot for as long as possible the glass should first be warmed.

Put a heaped teaspoon of sugar into the glass. Stir in a measure of Irish whiskey, then fill to within about 2.5 cm/1 inch of the top with *strong, hot* black coffee. Stir well, so that the sugar dissolves, as this plays a key part in ensuring that the cream remains on the top of the coffee and does not mix in with it.

Holding a dessertspoon over the coffee, with the back of the spoon pointing up, carefully pour over double cream, until it is about 1.25 cm/½ inch from the top of the glass. Serve at once.

Champagne

'Champagne is the only drink that leaves a woman beautiful after drinking it', adjured Madame de Pompadour, and this is just one of the many reasons why over the years Champagne has become 'the beautiful drink of beautiful people', symbolizing all that is elegant, gay, carefree—and expensive! Even dedicated abstainers find it hard to resist its allure, as George Bernard Shaw admitted in *Candida*: 'I am only a beer tee-totaller, not a Champagne tee-totaller.'

In historical terms, Cham-pagne is a compara-tively recent invention. The Champagne area of France, 100 miles north-east of Paris, has, despite its northerly position, produced excellent wines since Roman Times. Henry IV was so enamoured of them that he had his own presses there, to provide him with Ay wines—as they were also known— and Henry VIII retained a special commissioner in the region to ensure his continu-ous supply. But these were still wines, not the sparkling, effervescent, nectar of the gods we enjoy today. For this we owe our thanks to a French monk, Father Pierre Pérignon, better known as Dom Pérignon, whose name is revered by Cham-pagne producers and Champagne drink-ers throughout the world. For forty-five years, from 1670 until his death in 1715, Dom

Pérignon was the head cellarer at the Abbey of Hautvillers, a monastery which had always had a good reputation for its wine. The title cellarer gives little idea of how prestigious this position was, for it involved responsibility for the administration of the abbey's vineyards, as well as the making and selling of the wine, its chief source of revenue. The cellarer was also in charge of all the abbey's finances, and apart from the abbott, was considered to be the most important monk in the monastery.

The Secret of the Bubbles

Dom Pérignon discovered that by bottling in April the wine that he had made the previous autumn, a second fermentation took place inside the bottle, with the result that when the wine was opened it bubbled. It may seem strange that no-one had tried this earlier, but it was not until the late seventeenth century that glass bottles strong enough to withstand the pressure of fermentation were developed in England.

As a maritime nation with strong trading links with Spain, the English had been using cork for stoppering for some time, but in this land-locked area of France it had never been seen, until two Spanish monks on their way to Sweden stopped for a night at the Abbey de Hautvillers. What amazed their hosts was the extraordinary bark-like substance they used to stopper their water gourds. On being told all about cork and its properties, the monks informed Dom Pérignon, who instantly saw its value in the making of his wine. The clever monk is consequently as great a hero in north Catalonia, where cork is grown, as he is in Champagne, for he is universally given the credit for being the first man to use cork as a stopper for wine bottles.

Dom Pérignon's other great talent was that he perfected the art of blending wines. His successor to the position of cellarer wrote a pamphlet on the great man and in it he recorded that:

Father Pérignon did not taste the grapes in the vineyards, although he went out almost every day to inspect them as they approached maturity, but he arranged for samples to be brought to him and tasted them the next morning before breakfast, after they had spent the night on his window-ledge. He composed his blends not only according to the flavour of the juice but also according to what the weather had been like that year—an early or late development, depending on the amount of cold or rain there had been—and according to whether the vines had grown a rich or a mediocre foliage. All these factors served him for rules as to the composition of his blends.

During the second fermentation some sediment is formed and this must be removed if the end result is to be a beautiful clear wine.

After the wines have been left to mature, the bottles are turned upside down, so that the sediment rests on the cork. The original way of removing this was carefully to remove the cork, replace any wine that had been lost with the sediment and re-cork it. At the end of the nineteenth century a superior method was developed, whereby the wine in the neck of the bottle for about 2.5 cm/1 inch below the cork is frozen. The cork is then removed and out pops the now-frozen sediment, but with the loss of very little wine.

PINK CHAMPAGNE

Surprising as it may seem for a white wine—or golden wine as the Champenois prefer to describe it—Champagne is made from red grapes. To avoid the skin of the grape colouring the wine, special presses have to be used which are peculiar to Champagne. Treading the grapes has always been far too plebeian an exercise for the production of this wine!

Occasionally, in the past, the wine was accidentally tinged with pink, but pink Champagne is now highly fashionable and a limited quantity is deliberately allowed to take on the hue.

Why Champagne is Unique...

The 'methode champenoise' has been copied by other wine producers throughout the world and while there are many very good sparkling wines, and a few superb ones, they are *not* Champagne and there are two main reasons for this.

Firstly the land. The designated area in which grapes for Champagne can be grown is all lime-stone, which imparts its own special flavour to the grapes and controls the way they develop. The cellars in which the wine is made and matured are carved out of the chalk deep in the ground and this keeps them naturally cool.

Secondly the climate. Other than the vine-yards of England, this is the most northerly area in Europe in which grapes are grown, so the grapes do not have a good deal of sunshine to ripen them in a normal summer. Frosts occur suddenly and sharply in November and December and this kills the yeasts which cause fermentation so it ceases to ferment *before* all the sugar has been converted into alcohol. In April, when the weather is warmer, fermentation recommences, at which moment the wine is bottled.

KIR ROYALE

Named after Abbé Kir, the mayor of Dijon who was a Resistance fighter during the German occupation of France in the Second World War. Crème de cassis is produced mainly in the area around Dijon and the combination of the liqueur with white wine (Kir) or Champagne (Kir Royale) has been enjoyed in the region for many years.

6 × 5 ml spoons/6 tsp crème de cassis	1 bottle chilled Champagne or sparkling white wine*

Makes 6 glasses

Put 5 ml/1 tsp of the crème de cassis in the base of each of the six chilled wine glasses, top up with the Champagne or sparkling white wine and stir once or twice to mix. Serve at once.

*This is a good way of improving the flavour of slightly inferior Champagne or a good sparkling white wine.

RITZ CHAMPAGNE

On average the Ritz sells 3,000 cases, that is 36,000 bottles, of Champagne a year. Of this quantity, 2,500 cases are the Ritz's own Champagne, produced especially for the London and Paris Ritz by Albert Rivière, and the remaining 500 cases are a mixture of the well-known names of other Champagne houses.

BUCK'S FIZZ

Considered by many to be one of the finest ways to start the day—although equally as welcome at more conventional drinking times—this masterpiece was the invention of Colonel Buckmaster who founded Buck's Club in London. It certainly has the royal seal of approval for H.R.H. Prince Philip, Duke of Edinburgh, is on record as saying 'Champagne and orange juice is a great drink. The orange improves the Champagne. The Champagne definitely improves the orange.'

To make a good Buck's Fizz it is imperative to use freshly squeezed orange juice. Anything else is a waste of good Champagne.

| freshly squeezed orange juice | chilled Champagne |

A quarter fill a tulip glass with orange juice, then top up with chilled Champagne.

'She's no mistress of mine
That drinks not her wine
Or frowns at my friends' drinking notions;
If my heart thou wouldst gain
Drink thy flask of Champaign;
Twill serve thee for paint and love-potions.'
                    She Would If She Could,
                    Sir George Etherage 1668

BLACK VELVET

There are some who feel that the mixture of Champagne and Guinness is a sacrilegious waste of good Champagne, while others—the Irish in particular—consider it to be unsurpassed by any other combination. To accord the finished product its due, it should be served in a silver tankard or goblet.

| 150 ml/5 fl oz Champagne | 150 ml/5 fl oz Guinness |

Makes 300 ml/10 fl oz (1¼ cups)

Pour the Champagne into the tankard or goblet, then carefully add the Guinness and serve.

RITZ CHAMPAGNE COCKTAILS

THE CÉSAR RITZ

A cocktail the hotel's founder would have been proud of.

15 ml/½ fl oz Armagnac

15 ml/½ fl oz peach brandy

dash of grenadine

chilled Champagne

Mix the Armagnac, peach brandy and grenadine in a chilled Champagne flute or tulip glass. Top up with Champagne and decorate with a slice of fresh peach or nectarine.

THE HUNNIFORD

A tribute to Gloria Hunniford.

30 ml/1 fl oz fraise liqueur

15 ml/½ fl oz crème de cassis

15 ml/½ fl oz dry vermouth

15 ml/½ fl oz lemon juice

chilled Champagne

Mix the fraise liqueur, crème de cassis, vermouth and lemon juice in a chilled Champagne flute or tulip glass. Top up with Champagne and decorate with a Singapore orchid—or, failing this, with a slice of orange.

'Give me Champaign and fill it to the brim
I'll toast in bumpers evéry lovely limb.'

Lord Chesterfield

JACKIE GRANT

In collusion with Jackie's boyfriend, Bob Burton devised this romantic cocktail, to be presented on the eve of their engagement.

30 ml/1 fl oz fraise liqueur

15 ml/½ fl oz crème de mûres

30 ml/1 fl oz fresh lemon juice

dash of passion fruit nectar

chilled Champagne

Mix the fraise liqueur, crème de mûres, lemon juice and passion fruit nectar in a chilled Champagne flute or tulip glass. Top up with Champagne and decorate with half a strawberry.

ROYAL BLUSH

A cocktail devised by Bob Burton in 1986 to celebrate the marriage of His Royal Highness Prince Andrew, Duke of York, to Miss Sarah Ferguson.

15 ml/½ fl oz passion fruit liqueur

15 ml/½ fl oz crème de mûres

30 ml/1 fl oz fresh lemon juice

dash of dry vermouth

chilled Champagne

Put the passion fruit liqueur, crème de mûres, lemon juice and vermouth into a cocktail shaker and shake well. Strain into a chilled Champagne flute or tulip glass. Top up with Champagne and garnish with rose petals.

GOLDEN ARROW

Despite the eulogies written about the famous train, it never matched up to this.

15 ml/½ fl oz Cognac
30 ml/1 fl oz peach brandy

15 ml/½ fl oz dry vermouth
chilled Champagne

Mix the Cognac, peach brandy and vermouth in a chilled Champagne flute or tulip glass. Top up with Champagne and decorate with a slice of fresh peach or nectarine.

RITZ FIZZ

An exciting blue cocktail which lives up to its name.

a dash of amaretto
a dash of strained lemon juice

a dash of Blue Curaçao
chilled Champagne

Mix the amaretto, lemon juice and Curaçao together in a chilled Champagne flute or tulip glass. Top up with Champagne and decorate with a rose petal.

Cocktails and Aperitifs

There are countless theories as to exactly how the cocktail came into being. The French, who always like to lay claim to anything remotely connected with food and drink, maintain it is a French invention, since a mixture of Champagne and brandy, known as 'coquetel', was drunk in the Bordeaux area in the early part of the eighteenth century. Albeit the most plausible of all the explanations available, regrettably it has to be discounted for it seems certain that the cocktail originated on the other side of the Atlantic.

The earliest written reference appeared in an American periodical entitled 'The Balance', published on 13 May 1806, which stated that a 'cocktail is a stimulating liquor composed of spirits of any kind, sugar, water and bitters—it is vulgarly called "bittered sling"'. The drinking of 'slings' was certainly common practice at this time for Charles W Janson wrote in *The Stranger in America* in 1807, 'The first craving of an American in the morning is for ardent spirits mixed with sugar, mint, or some other hot herb, and which are called slings.'

Some say that the word 'cocktail' derives from the practice of 'docking' or cutting the tail of any horse that was not a pure thoroughbred, so that by definition a 'cocktail' was a mixture. However, the vast majority of the fables concerning the incarnation of the word 'cocktail' relate to a cockerel's plumage and cock-fighting in the Southern States where, by the end of the eighteenth century, the victorious bird would often be given an alcoholic concoction to try to improve its chances in the ensuing fight.

One Betsy Flanagan, who ran a hostelry popular with Washington's soldiers in Virginia back in 1779, is among several who are credited with being its creator. Adjacent to her establishment was a chicken farm whose proprietor was a pro-British Tory who became the butt of many a jest of the men as they drank in the bar. One evening they held a somewhat exuberant 'Tory chicken party' and, as the finale to the celebrations, Betsy prepared each of them one of her renowned, highly potent 'bracers'. They were poured into individual bottles and corked, and each cork was decorated with a feather from the tail of one of the unfortunate farmer's cockerels. Before opening their tipple, one of the officers, who happened to be French, proposed a toast with the immortal words 'Vive le Cocktail' and thus the cocktail was conceived— or so the story goes!

One of the most appealing tales concerns the beautiful daughter of King Axolotl VIII of Mexico. Her name was Xoctl and she used to prepare the most exquisite drinks for the Americans who came to her father's court (in between sparrings on the battlefield). Unable to pronounce her name the officers called both her, and her creations, Cocktails.

Whatever its early origins, the cocktail really came into its own in the United States during prohibition in the 1920s and '30s, as mixing drinks was about the only way of making bootleg alcohol palatable. Talullah Bankhead—a regular guest at the Ritz when in London—did more to popularize the cocktail than anyone else, for her fans emulated her every move, and it was not long before cocktails were being drunk, not only in the United States but throughout Europe. It is claimed that in the period between the First and Second World Wars, as many as 5,000 different cocktails were invented—some good, some bad and many indifferent.

*S*haken not Stirred, or Stirred not Shaken . . .

James Bond, alias Ian Fleming, preferred his martinis to be 'shaken not stirred', but the martini is in fact one of the very few drinks which can be made either by shaking or stirring, according to personal preference. The majority have to be prepared one way or the other— either shaken so that the flavours become thoroughly infused, or gently stirred so that the ingredients blend together without curdling, or the mixture becoming cloudy.

Shaking is far and away the more popular method, especially amongst barmen, for it gives them an opportunity to show off their prowess with a shaker—and inside every successful barman is a showman dying to get out. To make a 'shaken cocktail' the shaker should be quarter-filled with crushed ice, the cocktail ingredients added, the lid put on securely and the whole

BASIC EQUIPMENT

Cocktail shaker The majority of cocktails cannot be made without one. Most cocktail shakers are like mini vacuum flasks so that the ice, spirits and other ingredients stay cold inside, while the outside remains easy to handle.

A strainer These are usually flat with a coiled spring all the way round. Straining a cocktail is most important to prevent an excess quantity of ice diluting the finished article. Some cocktail shakers have a built-in strainer, but a separate strainer is still essential for stirred cocktails.

Mixing glass and spoon A large tumbler or small tankard can be used instead of a mixing glass, but a long-handled spoon is necessary so that the ingredients become properly stirred right down to the base.

Measures Accurate measuring is important and since most kitchen measuring jugs do not have a small enough scale, a set of small measures is vital.

An ice hammer and tongs While ice can be crushed with a rolling pin between the folds of a clean cloth, it is much easier to break it up with an ice hammer. Tongs make the handling of whole ice cubes much simpler.

An ice bucket Keeps both cubes and crushed ice frozen for some time.

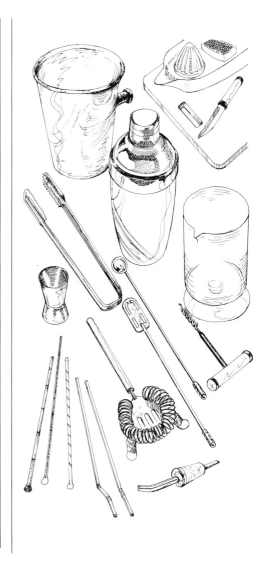

vigorously shaken. Intricate arm and body movements do nothing to improve the cocktail, although they can be fun to watch and if the shaker is also the consumer he (or she) then has the satisfaction of knowing they have earned their drink at the end of it! After shaking, the cocktail should be strained into glasses and served at once.

When a cocktail is stirred, a mixing glass or jug (according to the quantity being prepared) should be half-filled with crushed ice, the cocktail ingredients added and the mixture stirred with a long spoon so that all ingredients become thoroughly blended and chilled. The cocktail is then strained into glasses and served.

The Art of Making a Good Cocktail . . .

* Always use the finest ingredients, i.e. 40° proof London Dry gin or a good blended whisky, rather than their cheaper alternatives.

* Make sure you have plenty of crushed ice on hand—a good cocktail cannot be made without ice.

* Follow the instructions and quantities in a recipe *exactly*. In cooking it frequently does not matter if you use 1 tablespoon or 1½ tablespoons of an ingredient, but with cocktails it can alter the flavour dramatically.

* Gather together all the ingredients and equipment that you will need *before* you start mixing, including making any elaborate garnishes. A cocktail will spoil if half the ingredients are already in a shaker and you then start rummaging in the back of the drinks cupboard for a vital bottle.

* Always put the cheapest ingredients in first and finish with the most expensive. If you should make a mistake halfway through, at least you will not have to discard a healthy measure of the best Cognac or whisky!

* When making cocktails in a shaker, only half-fill the shaker so that all the ingredients become thoroughly shaken together and the ice chills them down quickly.

* Do not try to be economical and use the same ice again—even if making more of the same cocktail—for it will have started to melt.

* If a recipe says a cocktail should be stirred, stir it, if it says shake, then shake. If you reverse the method, you are likely to ruin a perfectly good drink.

* Chill glasses in the refrigerator for about 30 minutes before filling them.

Decorating Cocktails

Part of the glamour of a cocktail is the way in which it is served, so you should never stint on decoration. Certain cocktails are traditionally served in a particular shape of glass (see pages 18–19), but whatever their shape, cocktail glasses should always be clear so that you can see the elixir you are consuming.

Some cocktails, like a dry martini, demand the simplest adornment, such as a solitary olive or a twist of zest from a citrus fruit, while others, in particular the long, fruit-flavoured cocktails look sensational if decorated with fruit and flowers.

Virtually any fruit can be used, either cut in slices to decorate the side of the glass or placed on cocktail sticks in, or across, the glass. The only criterion is that the fruit chosen should complement, not fight, the flavours of the particular cocktail. Oranges, lemons, limes, strawberries and maraschino cherries are the most common, but fresh cherries, pineapple, kiwi fruit, nectarines, star fruit and melon cubes can all be used to decorate cocktails. In addition, cocktail garnishes may include slices of cucumber, sprigs of mint and borage or other mild herbs. Parasols and fancy 'swizzle sticks' also add a final frivolous flourish.

When it comes to flowers, there is virtually no end to the possibilities, although any flowers known to be poisonous should obviously be avoided. One or two smaller flowers generally look more elegant, and are more practical, than a large bloom. Position the flowers carefully on the rim of the glass.

WHITE LADY

A creation of Harry's New York Bar in Paris in 1911, this became one of the most fashionable drinks for ladies in both Europe and America between the wars.

30 ml/1 fl oz gin
15 ml/½ fl oz Cointreau
15 ml/½ fl oz fresh lemon juice
5 ml/1 tsp egg white

Put all the ingredients into a cocktail shaker with ice. Shake well, then strain into a cocktail glass and serve without any adornments.
Variation: The Pink Lady is made up of 60 ml/2 fl oz gin, 15 ml/½ fl oz grenadine and a dash of egg white.

SINGAPORE SLING

Created in 1915 by the head barman of Raffles Hotel in Singapore, Ngiam Tong Boon.

60 ml/2 fl oz gin
30 ml/1 fl oz cherry brandy
30 ml/1 fl oz fresh orange juice
30 ml/1 fl oz fresh lime juice
30 ml/1 fl oz fresh pineapple juice
1 dash Angostura bitters
1 dash Cointreau

Put all the ingredients into a shaker with ice and shake well. Strain into a tall or Collins glass, filled with ice. Decorate with a slice of fresh pineapple and a maraschino cherry and serve.

MARGARITA

Mexico's renowned cocktail made from tequila, which in Mexico is frequently drunk neat with a pinch of salt.

60 ml/2 fl oz tequila
15 ml/½ fl oz Cointreau
15 ml/½ fl oz fresh lime juice

Frost each glass with lime juice and salt (see page 20) and chill in the refrigerator for 15 minutes. Pour the tequila, Cointreau and lime juice into a cocktail shaker with ice. Shake well, then strain into the prepared glasses and serve.

THE SOUR

One of the great classics, comprising spirit, citrus juice, sugar and sometimes a little egg white as well. Whisky Sour, made with Bourbon or Canadian rye, is the original.

60 ml/2 fl oz Bourbon or rye
15 ml/½ fl oz lemon juice
7½ ml/¼ fl oz sugar syrup

If you wish, the glasses for this can be frosted with a little sugar. Put all the ingredients into a shaker with ice. Strain into chilled sour glasses, decorate with a twist of lemon zest and serve.

'Prohibition has made nothing but trouble.'

Al Capone

MINT JULEP

'I must descant a little upon the mint julep, as it is, with the thermometer at 100 degrees, one of the most delightful and insinuating potations that ever was invented, and may be drunk with equal satisfaction when the thermometer is as low as 70 degrees...' wrote the novelist and sailor Captain Marryat.

One of *the* great recipes from America's Deep South, the word is said to come from the Persian *gulab*, meaning rose water, and referred to a number of sweet, syrupy drinks served on both sides of the Atlantic.

the leaves of 2 large sprigs mint	60–90 ml/2–3 fl oz Bourbon
5 ml/1 tsp caster sugar	a dash of rum

Frost a long glass with sugar and place in the refrigerator. In a mixing glass press the mint leaves together with the sugar, using the handle of a wooden spoon, to bruise them. Add the Bourbon and rum and stir until the sugar has dissolved. Half-fill the glass with crushed ice. Strain over the julep and stir. Decorate with two additional mint sprigs.

DRY MARTINI

'I must get out of these wet clothes and into a Dry Martini.'

Alexander Wollcott (1887–1943)

The most famed cocktail of them all was invented in 1910 by a Signor Martini at The Old Knickerbocker Hotel, New York, for John D Rockerfeller. The proportion of vermouth to gin is open to discussion, but the 'drier' the martini required the less vermouth you should use. In a very dry martini some people prefer to replace the classic green olive with a twist of lemon zest.

60 ml/2 fl oz London Dry gin	15 ml/½ fl oz dry vermouth

Either put the gin and vermouth into a cocktail shaker with ice and shake vigorously as James Bond would wish, or—for those who fear this action 'bruises' the gin—pour into a mixing glass with ice, stir gently, then strain into a cocktail glass. Add a green olive or twist of lemon zest and serve.

'You can no more keep a martini in the refrigerator than you can keep a kiss there. The proper union of gin and vermouth ... is one of the happiest marriages on earth and one of the shortest-lived!'

The House, Bernard de Voto 1951

HARVEY WALLBANGER

There are conflicting stories as to exactly how this cocktail achieved its name. Certainly it was called after a surfer by the name of Tom Harvey who frequented Pancho's Bar on Manhattan Beach, California. But whether it was because, when he arrived in the bar each evening and ordered his own speciality of vodka, orange juice and Galliano liqueur, he banged his surfboard against the wall at the same time, or, having been defeated in an important surfing competition one day he drank rather too many to console himself and cannoned from wall to wall on the way out, is a matter open to conjecture!

60 ml/2 fl oz vodka
120 ml/4 fl oz fresh orange juice

15 ml/½ fl oz Galliano liqueur

Put the vodka and orange juice into a cocktail shaker with ice and shake well. Strain into a chilled, old-fashioned glass half-filled with ice. Carefully pour the Galliano liqueur over the back of a spoon held close to the surface of the cocktail, so that it floats on the surface. Serve with a straw.

RITZ SPECIALS

THE RED BOX

Designed for Cabinet Ministers.

45 ml/1½ fl oz sweet vermouth
15 ml/½ fl oz dry vermouth

45 ml/1½ fl oz dry white wine
15 ml/½ fl oz banana liqueur

Stir the ingredients together in a mixing glass. Fill a ballon glass with ice and strain the mixture over it. Decorate with a maraschino cherry.

SKI DOO

Only eccentrics would pop into the Ritz in their ski-wear, but there are some keen skiers among the hotel's clientèle.

75 ml/2½ fl oz dry white wine
15 ml/½ fl oz Cointreau
30 ml/1 fl oz quince liqueur

15 ml/½ fl oz dry vermouth
15 ml/½ fl oz Cinzano Bianco

Put three or four ice cubes into an old-fashioned glass. Pour the ingredients into the glass in the above order, then stir to mix. Decorate with a slice of orange and a cocktail stirrer.

PEACH OF A DRINK

A good pick-me-up at the end of the day.

40 ml/¼ fl oz Scotch whisky

30 ml/1 fl oz peach Schnapps

7½ ml/¼ fl oz vermouth

Stir the ingredients together in a mixing glass and strain either into an ice-filled old-fashioned glass or into a chilled martini glass. Decorate with a slice of peach or orange.

*L*ong Drinks

THE CHARLOTTE ROSE

45 ml/1½ fl oz Cognac

15 ml/½ fl oz amaretto

60 ml/2 fl oz fresh orange juice

15 ml/½ fl oz fresh lemon juice

Put all the ingredients into a cocktail shaker with ice and shake well. Fill a tall glass with ice, strain over the cocktail and garnish with a slice of orange. Serve with a straw.

THE IMPERIAL JADE

Decorate with a Singapore orchid to give that magical hint of the Orient.

30 ml/1 fl oz advocaat

30 ml/1 fl oz Blue Curaçao

15 ml/½ fl oz fresh lemon juice

75 ml/2½ fl oz fresh orange juice

Put all the ingredients into a cocktail shaker with ice and shake well. Strain into a tall glass filled with ice and decorate with a Singapore orchid. Serve with a straw.

THE CHANDLER

The sailing man's special.

30 ml/1 fl oz dark rum

30 ml/1 fl oz fresh lemon juice

45 ml/1½ fl oz passion fruit nectar

15 ml/½ fl oz Blue Curaçao

30 ml/1 fl oz dry vermouth

Put all the ingredients into a cocktail shaker with ice and shake well. Strain into a chilled sour glass and decorate with a slice of kiwi fruit.

*A*fter Dinner Cream Cocktails

COFFEE CREAM

A perfect post-dinner tipple.

7½ ml/¼ fl oz Malibu

15 ml/½ fl oz Kahlua

15 ml/½ fl oz banana liqueur

40 ml/1¼ fl oz double cream

Put the Malibu, Kahlua, banana liqueur and cream into a cocktail shaker with ice. Shake well, then strain into a martini glass. Float three coffee beans on the top.

HAZEL

It is sprinkled with grated hazelnuts before serving, but is this cocktail also the name of a girl?

30 ml/1 fl oz Frangelica
7½ ml/¼ fl oz orange liqueur
7½ ml/¼ fl oz Tia Maria
40 ml/1¼ fl oz double cream

Put the Frangelica, orange liqueur, Tia Maria and cream into a cocktail shaker with ice. Shake well, then strain into a martini glass. Decorate with grated hazelnuts.

———— APÉRITIFS ————

Most cocktails are served as apéritifs, but all apéritifs are not cocktails. Sherry, white wines, as well as straight spirits, vermouths and other fortified wines are all traditionally drunk before meals to sharpen the appetite—for that is the chief function of an apéritif.

Sherry

'The civilized drink' is how Somerset Maugham described sherry. Sadly, its image has taken a considerable buffeting in recent years and the word now tends to conjure up a vision of old ladies genteelly sipping a sweet mixture in Tunbridge Wells or Eastbourne. This is a pity, for a glass of chilled fino, or the drier manzanilla has few equals as an apéritif.

There are a variety of reasons for the decline in sherry drinking, but one of the most important has been the marketing of cheap imitations from Cyprus and South Africa. The genuine article, from Jerez, is produced with great care and under much stricter controls. Another factor is the change from drinking sweet wines to drier ones. Sherry is still stuck in many people's minds as an old-fashioned sweet drink, which is not the case.

There are two points to remember when drinking a glass of dry sherry as an apéritif. Firstly, the Spanish always serve it chilled, in the same way as a white wine, and this makes all the difference. Secondly, it should not be drunk out of the typical 'pub schooner' glass which gives no opportunity of appreciating its bouquet. A copita (see page 18) is a much more suitable glass, or failing that, a champagne tulip.

Vermouth

The Alpine regions of France and Italy are where the majority of European (and best known) vermouths are produced; the French version is the lighter and drier of the two.

The origins of vermouth date back to the Romans, who would macerate herbs in wine, both to improve their flavour and for medicinal purposes. The latter was one of the most important functions of the vermouths produced by monks in the Middle Ages. Methods of making vermouth vary, but in every case a mixture of herbs, spices and vegetable extracts, including camomile, quinine, vanilla and iris root amongst their ingredients, is macerated for six to twelve months in wine, which is sometimes distilled. The result is a drink which varies from a *very* dry white to a sweet, rich red.

Extensively used in cocktails, vermouths are also served on their own on the rocks, or with a dash of soda or carbonated mineral water as an apéritif. The mildly bitter after-taste helps to promote the flow of gastric juices, making the ensuing meal easier to digest.

'Teetotallers lack the sympathy and generosity of men that drink.'
    Shorter Lyrics of the 20th Century, W H Davies

'Nothing makes a woman look better than three cocktails inside a man.'
    Anon

Spirits

Man has been distilling spirits the world over, almost since the dawn of time. Simple to make, this cheap form of strong liquor has over the centuries had a lot to answer for, in terms of drunken debauchery. Cheap gin, known as 'mother's ruin', was the scourge of the eighteenth and nineteenth century in England.

Gin, distilled from grain and flavoured with juniper, and Scotch whisky, distilled from malted barley, have always been the two spirits most successfully made in Britain. Rum, the favoured drink of British sailors, has always had its followers in Europe, and once Christopher Columbus took sugar cane to the New World it flourished and quickly gained ascendancy there. Vodka, considered by many to be the purest of the spirits, remained the preserve of the Russians and the Slavs until modern times.

Scotch has always been drunk neat, the idea of adding water of any kind (including ice) to a blended whisky being anathema to a Scot—and to a malt whisky, pure sacrilege! Gin, on the other hand, with its more neutral flavour, responds well to being mixed, hence its great popularity in cocktails; even a gin and tonic, now the most usual way of serving gin, is in effect a cocktail.

Pink gin, the most popular drink for London's smart set between the wars, was a Royal Naval invention, made with gin, water and Angostura bitters. Its original use was medicinal, the bitters being manufactured from the bark of the Cusparia tree, well known as a cure for malaria and other tropical diseases.

One For The Road

'Water,' declared Andrew Boorde in 1542, 'is not wholesome, sole by itself, for an Englishman.' However, increased awareness of the dangers of drinking and driving, and indeed of other problems associated with excessive consumption of alcohol has, despite the eminent writer's stricture, resulted in us becoming a nation of mineral water drinkers.

Whatever its virtues, there is no escaping the fact that a glass of water, even when served with ice and a slice of lemon or lime, looks dull and puritanical, while a coloured concoction, exquisitely garnished, is a delight to both the eye and the palate—hence the increasing popularity of the non-alcoholic cocktail. Such a drink will psychologically lift the spirits, even though there are no spirits present.

Many reasons are given for abstinence—health and religion being the most predominant—but that supplied by Nancy Astor to the *Reader's Digest* in 1960 must surely be as good as any. 'One reason I do not drink is that I like to know when I am enjoying myself.' A fair observation for over two thousand years ago a Greek philosopher in the 7th century BC wrote 'I fear the man who drinks water and so remembers this morning what the rest of us said last night.'

PUSSYFOOT

This was the nickname of William E Johnson (1862–1945), a revenue officer during the years of prohibition, whose methods were, to say the least, stealthy—and the cocktail named after him is, naturally, free of alcohol.

30 ml/1 fl oz fresh orange juice

30 ml/1 fl oz fresh lemon juice

30 ml/1 fl oz fresh lime juice

½ an egg yolk

a dash of grenadine

Put all the ingredients into a cocktail shaker with ice. Shake well, then strain into a chilled cocktail glass. Decorate with a cocktail cherry and serve.

THE BABY BRETT

Created for the television mini-series 'The Bretts'.

30 ml/1 fl oz passion fruit nectar

30 ml/1 fl oz lemon squash

60 ml/2 fl oz fresh orange juice

1 teaspoon fresh lemon juice

Put all the ingredients into a cocktail shaker with ice. Pour into a wine glass filled with ice and decorate with a slice of kiwi fruit.

> 'Drink to me only with thine eyes
> And I will pledge with mine
> Or leave a kiss but in the cup
> And I'll not look for wine.'
>
> Ben Jonson

THE SHIRLEY TEMPLE

Designed for children, but enjoyed by adults.

a dash of grenadine   chilled ginger ale

Pour the grenadine into the base of a chilled Champagne flute or tulip glass. Top up with chilled ginger ale. Decorate with two cocktail cherries and serve.

LEMONADE

'The Persian's Heaven is easily made,
'Tis but black eyes and Lemonade!'
        attributed to Sir Thomas More (1478–1535)

The British horror of the Muslim laws of abstinence is very apparent in the above and clearly More did not rate this beverage very highly, but few drinks are more refreshing on a hot summer's day.

4 lemons   150 ml/5 fl oz water

100 g/4 oz white sugar

Makes 4–6 glasses

Peel the zest from one of the lemons and put into a small, heavy-based saucepan. Add the sugar and water and put over a low heat until the sugar has dissolved, stirring frequently. Increase the heat, bring to the boil and boil for 2 minutes, then remove from the heat and allow to cool.

Squeeze the juice from all the lemons and stir into the sugar syrup. Strain into a jug and chill.

To serve, put two or three ice cubes into a tall glass, one-third fill with the lemonade mixture, then top up with water, soda water or carbonated mineral water. Garnish each glass with a slice of lemon and a sprig of mint.

Note: The undiluted mixture can be used in cocktails and will keep for several days in the refrigerator.

TEA LIME PUNCH

3 tea bags   juice of 3 limes

450 ml/15 fl oz boiling   grated rind of 2 lemons
        water
                            caster sugar to taste

Makes 4–6 glasses

Put the tea bags into a heatproof jug and pour over the boiling water. Add the juice of the limes, grated rind of the lemons and the sugar. Steep for 3 minutes. Strain and chill. Serve in tall glasses with ice and sprigs of mint.

STRAWBERRY SPECIAL

A sensational strawberry cocktail, which is almost as thick as a sorbet.

4 fresh strawberries	15 ml/½ fl oz strawberry syrup
15 ml/½ fl oz fresh orange juice	250 ml/8 fl oz crushed ice
1 teaspoon fresh lime juice	

Put all the ingredients into a blender and purée until smooth, but do not over-mix or it will become too runny. Pour into a bowl glass and decorate with a half strawberry and a slice of orange.

THE PADDINGTON BEAR

No marmalade, but Paddington's favourite ingredient, i.e. oranges.

105 ml/3½ fl oz fresh orange juice	15 ml/½ fl oz fresh lime juice
30 ml/1 fl oz fresh grapefruit juice	2 teaspoons orgeat syrup

Put all the ingredients into a cocktail shaker with ice. Pour into a tall glass filled with ice and decorate with a slice of orange and a glacé cherry.

A FRUIT SPECTACULAR

Peach and passion fruit nectar are combined here with orange, lemon and pineapple juice to make an exciting elixir.

15 ml/½ fl oz peach nectar	15 ml/½ fl oz fresh lemon juice
45 ml/1½ fl oz passion fruit nectar	30 ml/1 fl oz pineapple juice
45 ml/1½ fl oz fresh orange juice	a dash of grenadine

Put all the ingredients, except the grenadine, into a cocktail shaker with ice. Pour into an old-fashioned tumbler half-filled with ice. Pour the grenadine on top and decorate with a slice of peach.

PEACHES AND GINGER

4 large peaches	½ tsp powdered ginger
4 oz raspberries	juice of 2 lemons
4 oz sugar	ginger beer
juice of 2 small oranges	

Makes 4 glasses

Pare and stone the peaches, chop them coarsely and blend to a purée with the raspberries, sugar, juices and seasoning. Refrigerate for 30 minutes. Serve in tall glasses over cracked ice diluted equal amounts of ginger beer. Decorate with a slice of peach and an orange slice.

Punches

The word punch is said to come from the Hindi, 'panch' meaning five, for it was made of five essential ingredients—arrack, lime, sugar, spices and water—and was introduced to Britain in the seventeenth century by merchants with the East India Company. Over the years, however, through general usage, the word has loosely come to mean any drink made up in large quantities and served from a jug or bowl with a ladle. It includes mulled wine and hot spiced toddies as well as long, cool drinks.

In the Elizabethan era a famed potion was 'hippocras', a blend of red wine, ginger and honey, which would be strained through a cloth prior to consumption. It was also common to flavour wine with sage and other aromatic herbs, largely to disguise its poor quality and vinegary flavour. This problem of inferior wines explains why Shakespeare, in the guise of Sir John Falstaff, advised his audiences to 'forswear thin potations and addict themselves to sack', for sack, or sherris-sack as it was also known, from Jerez in Spain, being fortified with brandy, travelled better, and so came into Britain in a superior condition to most other wines from Europe.

Wassailing—from the Anglo-Saxon 'Waes Hael' meaning

Be Healthy—was a popular pastime during the Christmas period for centuries. Groups of people, in particular the young men of a village or town, roamed the streets carrying a large bowl and, knocking on the doors of the wealthier members of the parish, would demand their bowl be filled. More often than not, in the season of goodwill, and especially if they sang a song, the revellers would be rewarded with some mulled ale.

'Mull' is described in the dictionary as to 'warm, sweeten and spice' and the warming part of the operation would sometimes be carried out by simply plunging a hot poker from the fire into the drink. Alternatively a cone-shaped copper beer-warmer would be kept by the kitchen range for the sole purpose of heating the ale. In the Middle Ages mulled ales thickened with eggs and/or oatmeal would be consumed for breakfast and as a nightcap.

Indeed both thickened and spiced mulled ales remained popular up until the turn of this century. Mulled ale would often be served at the end of a party or ball to keep guests warm on the way home in their open carriages while thickened ale, almost like an alcoholic soup, was deemed to be recuperative fare for invalids and for mothers immediately after they had given birth. One William Fleming, who resided in the Lake District, recorded in his diary in 1818 the festivities among the other women which accompanied childbirth in the area. 'The Wife of a Farmer of mine was brought to Bed a few days ago and Preparations had been made previous to the expected event. As soon as the good Woman had been delivered, some Ale was put on the Fire with Spices to warm and Cheese . . . of which all present ate heartily and drank the warm Ale mixed with Rum or Brandy after which the married Women leapt over a Besom or Birch Broom and she who did not clear the Broom was pronounced the next for the Straw.'

The other favoured remedy for the sick and for nursing mothers was a posset: hot sweetened and spiced milk curdled with either ale or wine. In the seventeenth and eighteenth centuries, two-handled posset pots were made, with a spout starting from the base to ensure that the invalid drank the most nourishing part of the beverage. Some beautiful glass and porcelain examples of these can be seen in certain prestigious collections.

'A sparing diet did her health assure
Or sick, a posset was her cure.'

Dryden

PERFECT PUNCHES

* On no account must hot punch be allowed to boil or the alcohol will evaporate. Keep just below simmering point.

* Always use whole spices, such as cinnamon, nutmeg and cloves, and either strain the mixture before serving or tie the spices in a muslin bag and remove it before serving. Ground spices should not be used, for they render the drink cloudy and give it a grainy texture.

* When serving hot punches, always warm the goblet or bowl before adding the punch, so that it remains as hot as possible.

* To chill cold drinks in a punch bowl, use one large block of ice. Ice cubes will melt quickly in a large quantity of liquid and then cease to chill it, as well as diluting the punch unnecessarily.

THE BISHOP

This drink is often associated with Oxford and Cambridge undergraduates—presumably because they have always been somewhat short of funds and at one time it was one of the cheapest drinks they could prepare. Some recipes use a roasted lemon in the punch instead of an orange.

6 cloves	$\frac{1}{2}$ a nutmeg
1 orange	1.5 cm/$\frac{1}{2}$-inch piece dried ginger
300 ml/10 fl oz water	
5 cm/2-inch piece cinnamon stick	juice 1 lemon
	1 bottle port
4 allspice berries	50 g/2 oz/$\frac{1}{4}$ cup sugar

Oven: 350°F/180°C/Mark 4
Makes about 10 glasses

Stick the cloves into the orange. Put into the oven and bake for 30 minutes. Meanwhile put the water into a pan with the cinnamon, allspice berries, nutmeg and ginger. Bring to the boil and then boil gently for about 10 minutes.

Strain the water and the lemon juice into a clean pan. Add the port and roasted orange and heat gently together for about 10 minutes. Add the sugar and stir until the sugar has dissolved, then ladle into a heated punch bowl and serve at once.

'Let schoolmasters puzzle their brain,
With grammar, and nonsense, and learning,
Good liquor, I stoutly maintain,
Gives genius a better discerning.'
        She Stoops to Conquer, Oliver Goldsmith

'This ancient Silver bowl of mine, it tells of
   good old times.
Of joyous days and jolly nights, and merry
   Christmas Chimes.
They were a free and jovial race, but honest,
   brave and true,
That dipped their ladle in the punch when
   this old bowl was new.'

Oliver Wendell Holmes

HOT WHISKEY

A drink offered in almost every bar in Ireland,
but rarely seen elsewhere.

2 cloves	5 ml/1 tsp sugar
1 thick slice of lemon	60 ml/2 fl oz whiskey
a pinch of ground cinnamon	boiling water

Stick the cloves into the slice of lemon. Put the
cinnamon, sugar and whiskey into a heated
whiskey tumbler and stir lightly. Add the lemon.
Pour over the boiling water, stir well and leave
to infuse for 2–3 minutes before drinking.

MULLED ALE

A tot of brandy added to this thickened mulled ale will warm the cockles of your heart on a cold winter's night.

2 eggs	¼ of a nutmeg
600 ml/1 pint/20 fl oz bitter or light ale	20 ml/4 tsp sugar
0.75 cm/¼-inch piece dried ginger	30 ml/1 fl oz brandy (optional)

Makes 2 × 300 ml/½ pint/1¼ cup tankards

Beat the eggs with 4 tablespoons of the bitter or light ale in a large bowl. Put the remaining bitter, ginger, nutmeg and sugar into a saucepan and heat gently together for 10 minutes without boiling. Remove from the heat and leave to cool for about 2 minutes.

Discard the nutmeg and ginger, pour over the eggs, beating all the time. Return to the saucepan and heat gently for a further 2–3 minutes, stirring continually. While stirring take great care not to curdle the eggs. Stir in the brandy if using, then ladle into punch glasses and serve.

PLANTERS' PUNCH

Redolent of the Caribbean, this is the classic Jamaican rum punch. The original recipe called for the proportions to be 'one of sour, two of

'I got up to The Peacock where I found everybody drinking hot punch in self-preservation.'
The Holly Tree Inn, Charles Dickens

sweet, three of strong and four of weak', i.e. one part fresh lime juice, two parts sugar, three parts rum and four parts water or crushed ice.

90 ml/3 fl oz lime juice	300 ml/10 fl oz soda water or carbonated mineral water
270 ml/9 fl oz white rum	
175 g/6 oz caster sugar	

Makes 4–6 glasses

Mix the lime juice and rum together in a jug. Add the sugar and stir until it is dissolved. Pour in the soda water or carbonated mineral water and stir.

Half-fill 4–6 glasses with crushed ice and decorate each glass with a slice of fresh pineapple and a slice of lime. Pour in the punch and serve.

THE PUNCH UP

A warming punch for winter evenings.

3 bottles claret	½ a nutmeg
750 ml/1¼ pints/3 cups water	6 cloves
250 ml/8 fl oz Cognac	2 lemons, sliced
150 ml/5 fl oz peach brandy	1 orange, sliced
3 cinnamon sticks	sugar to taste

Makes about 36 glasses

Put the wine, water, Cognac, peach brandy, cinnamon sticks, nutmeg, cloves, lemon and orange slices into a pan and heat gently for 20 minutes. Add sugar to taste and serve.

BONAPARTE'S PUNCH

Mandarin Napoleon, a liqueur based on tangerines, gives this punch an added kick.

3 bottles dry white wine	juice of 2 lemons
150 ml/5 fl oz fresh orange juice	sugar to taste
250 ml/8 fl oz Mandarin Napoleon	*To decorate:*
	1 lemon, sliced
250 ml/8 fl oz Cognac	1 orange, sliced
300 ml/10 fl oz soda or carbonated mineral water	about 6 strawberries, sliced

Makes approx 32 glasses

Mix together the wine, orange juice, Mandarin Napoleon and Cognac. Add sugar to taste and stir until it has dissolved. Pour into a punch bowl or jug and add the orange and lemon slices and the sliced strawberries. Refrigerate until just before serving, then add the soda or mineral water and stir well.

BROWN BETTY

'Brown sugar, dissolved in 1 pint of hot water, a slice of lemon in it. Add cloves, cinnamon, brandy and a quart of strong ale. Heat it up and float a round of brown toast on top of it—and on the toast grate nutmeg and ginger root. Serve hot.'

Oxford Nightcaps, 1827

Appetizers

Eating and drinking have gone hand in hand ever since we can remember, and drinking (in moderation) has generally been considered as healthy a pursuit as eating. In the Bible, we are told in Psalms that 'Wine maketh glad the heart of man', while in Timothy we are admonished to 'Drink no longer water, but use a little wine for thy stomach's sake.' And one should not forget that Christ himself turned water into wine to enliven the proceedings at a wedding feast.

At a meal, the drink is selected to accompany the food and, on the whole, wine is usually considered to be the most suitable drink to serve with dinner. There are exceptions, such as drinking lager with curry or vodka with caviar, but no matter what the choice of menu, care is exercised in choosing the drinks to accompany— rather than dominate—the food.

The same should apply in reverse when making appetizers to serve with drinks. For example, while sweet dishes are rapidly gaining social ascendancy and are a superb accompaniment to Champagne, white wine or fruit-based cocktails, they are anathema to a dry martini or Bloody Mary, or even a gin and tonic. A twentieth-century invention for serving at 'drinks parties', at one time appetizers were just that—little tidbits to keep hunger at bay and whet the appetite prior to lunch or dinner. Increasingly though they are becoming a guest's hors d'oeuvre, if not their main course, as well as acting as 'blotting paper' to ward off inebriation, so a few slightly more substantial items are often appreciated.

Above all, they must be easy to eat—literally one or two mouthfuls—without involving sticky or greasy fingers. If serving sauces or dips do not make them too runny—no matter how good they taste, no-one is going to thank you when it drips down the front of their new designer number!

FILO MONEYBAGS

Quick and easy to prepare, these little 'bags' of filo pastry filled with blue Brie or Cambazola are always popular.

──METRIC/IMPERIAL── •	──CUP MEASURES──
450 g/1 lb blue Brie or Cambazola	1 lb Cambazola
400 g/14 oz filo pastry	14 oz filo pastry
75 g/3 oz butter, melted	6 tbsp/¾ stick butter, melted

Oven: 425°F/220°C/Mark 7
Makes 36

Cut the rind off the Brie or Cambazola and cut the cheese into 36 pieces; try to keep these as square as possible. Lay the pastry out on a working surface and brush with a clean brush to remove as much flour as possible. Cut the pastry into 72 × 7.5 cm/3-inch squares.

Take two pieces of pastry and brush 2.5 cm/1 inch all the way round their edges on both sides with melted butter. Keeping the two pastry squares together, place a piece of cheese in the centre, then bring up the edges and twist to enclose the cheese.

Place on a flat, non-stick baking sheet. Repeat with the remaining pastry squares and pieces of cheese. Place in the pre-heated oven and bake for 5 minutes or until golden brown. Serve hot.

> 'He that eateth well, drinketh well, he that drinketh well, sleepeth well; he that sleepeth well, sinneth not, he that sinneth not goeth straight through Purgatory to Paradise.'
> William Lithgow, 1609

BELGIAN SCALLOPS

A novel way of serving cocktail snacks is in little Chinese soup ladles. As they have a flat base they sit easily on a tray and can be filled with a variety of ingredients. People can help themselves to a spoon and, once they have eaten, simply replace it on another, or different part of, the tray.

──METRIC/IMPERIAL── •	──CUP MEASURES──
10 large scallops	10 large scallops
30 ml/2 tbsp balsamic vinegar	2 tbsp balsamic vinegar
15 ml/1 tbsp rapeseed oil	1 tbsp rapeseed oil
10 ml/2 tsp finely chopped tarragon	2 tsp finely chopped tarragon
salt and freshly milled black pepper	salt and freshly milled black pepper
20 tiny sprigs tarragon to garnish	20 tiny sprigs tarragon to garnish

Makes 20

Cut the scallops in half horizontally and put into a shallow dish. Mix together all the remaining ingredients, pour over the scallops and leave to marinate for at least 30 minutes or for up to 2 hours.

Drain the scallops and pour the marinade into a small saucepan. Place over a gentle heat. Heat a griddle or a large non-stick frying pan. Add the scallops and cook quickly for 2–3 minutes on one side, then turn and cook on the second side.

Lift out of the pan and place each one in a warmed Chinese ladle. Add the cooking juices to the marinade, and pour a teaspoonful of the liquid over each scallop. Garnish each with a tiny sprig of tarragon and serve.

GOUGÈRE

A speciality of Burgundy in France, this rich cheese choux pastry is served at wine tastings in the region to freshen the palate. Traditionally gougère is baked in a ring and then cut into slices, but when serving with drinks it is easier to eat if baked in small buns.

──METRIC/IMPERIAL── •	──CUP MEASURES──
100 g/4 oz plain flour	1 cup all-purpose flour
1.25 ml/¼ tsp salt	¼ tsp salt
freshly milled black pepper	freshly milled black pepper
200 ml/8 fl oz milk	1 cup milk
75 g/3 oz unsalted butter	6 tbsp/¾ stick butter
175 g/6 oz Gruyère cheese, finely grated	1 cup finely grated Gruyère cheese
4 eggs	4 eggs

Oven: 425°F/220°C/Mark 7
Makes about 36

Sift the flour and salt on to a piece of greaseproof paper and add the pepper. Put the milk and butter into a pan and bring slowly to the boil. Remove from the heat and add the flour all at once. Beat well, and if necessary return the pan to a very low heat until the mixture forms a ball that leaves the sides of the pan clean.

Remove from the heat and beat in all but 25 g/1 oz (⅙ cup) of the cheese. Beat thoroughly, then beat in the eggs one at a time, beating well after each addition.

Pile rounded teaspoonfuls of the mixture on to baking parchment on baking sheets, spacing them about 5 cm/2 inches apart to allow for spreading. It will probably be necessary to bake the mixture in two batches. Sprinkle each one with a little of the remaining cheese. Bake for 10–12 minutes in the pre-heated oven or until well-risen and a rich golden brown.

Remove from the oven, place on a heated serving dish and serve as soon as possible.

MINI SPINACH AND SMOKED SALMON ROULADES

Slices of these on a platter garnished with sprigs of watercress look truly 'Ritzy'.

——METRIC/IMPERIAL—— •	——CUP MEASURES——
For the roulade:	*For the roulade:*
175 g/6 oz spinach	6 oz spinach
salt	salt
25 g/1 oz butter	2 tbsp/¼ stick butter
25 g/1 oz flour	¼ cup all-purpose flour
300 ml/½ pint milk	1¼ cups milk
25 g/1 oz grated Parmesan cheese	⅙ cup grated Parmesan cheese
2 eggs, separated	2 eggs, separated
salt and freshly milled black pepper	salt and freshly milled black pepper
For the filling:	*For the filling:*
50 g/2 oz smoked salmon pieces	2 oz smoked salmon pieces
100 g/4 oz curd cheese	½ cup curd cheese
a squeeze of lemon juice	a squeeze of lemon juice
watercress sprigs to garnish	watercress sprigs to garnish

Oven: 400°F/200°C/Mark 6
Makes approx 32 slices

Line a 32.5 × 25 cm/13 × 10 inch Swiss roll tin with baking parchment. Wash the spinach and remove any stalks. Cook in 4 tablespoons boiling salted water until tender. Drain thoroughly, then chop finely.

Melt the butter in a pan, add the flour and cook for a minute. Gradually stir in the milk and bring to the boil, stirring all the time. Remove from the heat and stir in the spinach and cheese. Season to taste with salt and pepper. Beat in the egg yolks one at a time.

Whisk the egg whites until they form soft peaks, then fold into the mixture. Pour into the prepared tin and bake in the pre-heated oven for about 10 minutes or until golden brown. Remove from the oven and cut the roulade in half lengthways with sharp knife.

Turn out of the tin on to a piece of clean baking parchment, and carefully peel off the backing paper. Cut the fresh sheet of paper in half and roll up the two roulades lengthways, keeping the paper inside them. Put on one side and leave to cool.

Place the smoked salmon pieces in a food processor and process until smooth. Add the curd cheese and process again, then season to taste with lemon juice and salt and pepper.

Unroll the two roulades and spread each of them with half the filling. Re-roll, then cut each one into slices about 1 cm/⅓ inch thick. Place on a serving platter and garnish with watercress.

CHICKEN SATAY WITH PEANUT SAUCE

Mini satay sticks make an ideal nibble to serve with drinks.

METRIC/IMPERIAL	CUP MEASURES
450 g/1 lb chicken breast fillets	1 lb chicken breast fillets
30 ml/2 tbsp dry sherry	2 tbsp dry sherry
45 ml/3 tbsp light soy sauce	3 tbsp light soy sauce
30 ml/2 tbsp sesame oil	2 tbsp sesame oil
finely grated rind and juice 1 lemon	finely grated rind and juice 1 lemon
15 ml/1 tbsp sesame seeds	1 tbsp sesame seeds
For the sauce:	*For the sauce:*
25 g/1 oz creamed coconut	2 tbsp creamed coconut
100 ml/4 fl oz hot water	$\frac{1}{2}$ cup hot water
50 g/2 oz crunchy peanut butter	4 tbsp crunchy peanut butter
2.5 ml/$\frac{1}{2}$ tsp mild chilli powder	$\frac{1}{2}$ tsp mild chilli powder
2.5 ml/$\frac{1}{2}$ tsp soft brown sugar	$\frac{1}{2}$ tsp soft brown sugar
5 ml/1 tsp light soy sauce	1 tsp light soy sauce
10 ml/2 tsp very finely chopped onion	2 tsp very finely chopped onion

Makes about 30

Cut the chicken breast fillets into cubes approximately 1 cm/$\frac{1}{3}$ inch in size. Thread three cubes on to cocktail sticks and place in a shallow dish. Mix together all the remaining ingredients, pour over the satay sticks and leave to marinate for at least 4 hours or overnight.

Place the creamed coconut in a small pan with the water and heat gently until the coconut has melted. Stir in all the remaining sauce ingredients until they become well amalgamated, then remove the sauce from the heat, cover with clingwrap and leave to cool. Turn into a small bowl and stand it in the centre of a heated serving dish.

Place the satay sticks under a hot grill and grill for about 10 minutes, until they are golden brown and cooked through, turning once and basting with the remains of the marinade. Arrange the sticks on the serving dish so that it is easy for everyone to dip a stick into the sauce and then eat it.

Note: If it is easier the sticks can be cooked in a very hot oven for about 15 minutes, or they can be grilled earlier and reheated in a hot oven for 5 minutes.

STILTON WALNUTS

For this recipe you need to buy good quality walnut halves and the best source of these is generally a health food store.

METRIC/IMPERIAL	CUP MEASURES
125 g/5 oz Stilton	5 oz Stilton or other blue cheese
125 g/5 oz curd cheese	$\frac{5}{8}$ cup curd cheese
275 g/10 oz walnut halves	2$\frac{1}{2}$ cups walnut halves

Makes about 50

Crumble the Stilton and mash with the curd cheese. Use the cheese mixture to sandwich together two walnut halves.

STUFFED CHERRY TOMATOES

When served on a silver platter these tomatoes look sensational, for the red of the tomatoes is reflected in the silver. To be quite certain that they stand upright, *a very thin slice* can be cut off the base.

METRIC/IMPERIAL •	CUP MEASURES
500 g/1 lb 2 oz cherry tomatoes (approx 50)	1 lb 2 oz cherry tomatoes (approx 50)
salt	salt
150 ml/¼ pint thick mayonnaise	⅝ cup thick mayonnaise
50 g/2 oz fresh white breadcrumbs	½ cup fresh white breadcrumbs
50 g/2 oz white crabmeat	2 oz white crabmeat
50 g/2 oz brown crabmeat	2 oz brown crabmeat
freshly milled black pepper	freshly milled black pepper
dash Tabasco	dash Tabasco
tiny sprigs of dill to garnish	tiny sprigs of dill to garnish

Makes about 50

Cut the tops off the tomatoes and scoop out the pulp and seeds with a sharp coffee spoon; this can be used to flavour soups, stocks, casseroles

etc. Sprinkle the inside of each tomato with a little salt, then turn upside down on a piece of absorbent kitchen paper and leave for at least 20 minutes, but no longer than 1 hour.

Turn the mayonnaise into a basin and stir in the breadcrumbs and crabmeat. Add salt, black pepper and Tabasco to taste. Spoon the mixture into the tomato cases and arrange on a serving platter. Garnish each one with a tiny sprig of fresh dill.

PIGNATELLES

These Italian savouries are so-called because when they are cooked they puff up and resemble fir cones. They are at their best served freshly cooked, but the mixture can be made up several hours before it is required.

METRIC/IMPERIAL •	CUP MEASURES
450 g/1 lb potatoes	1 lb potatoes
salt	salt
65 g/2½ oz plain flour	⅜ cup plain flour
50 g/2 oz butter	4 tbsp/½ stick butter
150 ml/¼ pint water	⅝ cup water
3 eggs	3 eggs
175 g/6 oz strong Cheddar cheese, grated	1½ cups strong Cheddar cheese, grated
50 g/2 oz garlic sausage, very finely chopped	2 oz garlic sausage, very finely chopped
freshly milled black pepper	freshly milled black pepper
deep oil for frying	deep oil for frying

Makes 50

Scrub the potatoes, but do not peel them. Cook in boiling salted water until tender, then drain

> 'He that drinks well, does sleep well,
> He that sleeps well, doth think well,
> He that thinks well, doth do well,
> He that does well, must drink well.'
> Loyal Garland Song, 1686—Anon

and when cool enough to handle, peel and sieve. Sift the flour and a pinch of salt on to a piece of greaseproof paper.

Put the butter and water into a pan and heat gently until the butter has melted, then bring to the boil. Add the flour all at once, while the pan is still on a low heat. Beat well until the mixture forms a soft ball that leaves the sides of the pan clean. Remove from the heat and allow to cool slightly, then beat in the eggs, one at a time. When the mixture is thick and smooth, beat in the potato purée, then the cheese and garlic sausage. Season to taste.

Heat the oil and when hot, drop in teaspoonfuls of the mixture. Cook until they are golden brown and puffed up, remove with a draining spoon and dry on kitchen paper. Serve as soon as possible after cooking.

MINI PAVLOVAS

It is becoming increasingly chic to serve a few sweet items towards the end of a drinks party. At the Ritz they sometimes serve them around a small pot of dry ice which, in addition to keeping the food cold, billows out wafts of 'smoke' engendering an air of excitement.

Named after the ballerina Anna Pavlova, who danced at the Ritz, the Pavlova is an Australian creation and the secret is that it should be crisp on the outside, but have the consistency of marshmallow inside.

——METRIC/IMPERIAL——	——CUP MEASURES——
2 egg whites	2 egg whites
125 g/5 oz caster sugar	$\frac{5}{8}$ cup granulated sugar
2.5 ml/$\frac{1}{2}$ tsp bicarbonate of soda	$\frac{1}{2}$ tsp bicarbonate of soda
2.5 ml/$\frac{1}{2}$ tsp vinegar	$\frac{1}{2}$ tsp vinegar
200 ml/8 fl oz double cream	1 cup heavy cream
approx 12 large strawberries or 4 kiwi fruit	approx 12 large strawberries or 4 kiwi fruit

Oven: 300°F/150°C/Mark 2
Makes approx 24

Whisk the egg whites until they form stiff peaks, then gradually beat in the sugar a teaspoon at a time. Sift in the bicarbonate of soda and beat in, then beat in the vinegar.

Line two baking sheets with baking parchment and put about 24 teaspoonfuls of the mixture on the parchment, spacing them fairly well apart to allow for spreading. Flatten them with a palette knife. Put into the preheated oven and bake for about 20 minutes until they are just crisp. Remove from the oven, place on a wire rack and leave to cool.

Whip the cream until it holds its shape. Cut the strawberries in half or peel the kiwi fruit and cut into about 6 slices. Turn the pavlovas over and spread the underneath of each of them with a little of the cream. Top with half a strawberry or a slice of kiwi fruit.

Lay on a serving dish, trimming a little off the top (which is now the base) if necessary, to ensure they stand upright.

> '... in January 1934 The Prince of Wales's mistress, the American Lady Furness, decided to make a trip to the United States. In her book Double Exposure, Lady Furness tells how she had lunch at the Ritz with her friend Mrs Ernest Simpson on the day before she sailed. On hearing of Lady Furness's forthcoming absence from the scene, Mrs Simpson said: "Oh, Thelma, the little man is going to be so lonely."
>
> "Well, dear," replied Lady Furness, "you look after him while I'm away. See that he doesn't get into mischief."
>
> As Lady Furness noted sarcastically in her memoirs: "It was later evident that Wallis took my advice all too literally."'
>
> The London Ritz,
> Hugh Montgomery-Massingberd and
> David Watkin

The Morning After

'Waked this morning with my head in a sad taking through last night's drink which I am very sorry for. So rose and went out with Mr Creed to drink our morning draught, which he did give me in chocolate to settle my stomach,' wrote Samuel Pepys the morning following the coronation of Charles II in 1660.

However, as John Selden observed in *Table Talk*, 'Tis not the drinking that is to be blamed, but the excess'. An adage it is wise to remember the night before rather than the morning after, as it is only too easy for those few extra glasses that do the damage to slip down, almost unnoticed, when drinks and conversation are flowing in equal proportions. 'Never mix the grape with the grain' is another piece of sage advice, for it is the mixture of drinks which frequently causes both stomach and liver to rebel. No matter how good our intentions may be though, there are few of us who have not suffered at some time from over-indulgence the night before and there are any number of favoured cures. The best known (and by all accounts most successful) is the 'hair of the dog', which, while it may set you on the road to apparently instant recovery, can be a somewhat dangerous path to follow! Some alternatives are:

* Hot chocolate: Pepys' potion can be beneficial, for the chocolate itself contains iron and other minerals, the milk will provide a lining for the stomach and some much needed protein, and the sugar gives carbohydrate for energy.

* Coffee: Some find a cup of coffee helpful, but others find that it irritates the stomach and makes them feel even worse.

* China tea: Copious quantities of liquid enable the body to rehydrate and set about the task of repairing the damage that has been inflicted upon it, so weak China tea, with an added squeeze of lemon to provide Vitamin C, definitely helps.

* Bouillon: A cup of hot bouillon or vegetable or beef extract is a savoury cure which helps some.

* Food: If it can be faced, an old-fashioned cooked breakfast will do much to restore the body's metabolism and return it to its usual equilibrium. Some swear by hot, spicy foods. If the idea of bacon, eggs and sausages is unappealing, then have some cereal, muesli or toast. Fresh fruit can be good, but may be too acid for a malady brought about by wine.

* Fernet Branca: Italian bitters, made from vegetables, which are 40 percent proof, made into a long drink with soda or mineral water. This is reputed to be one of the best headache cures in the world—though opinions differ as to its palatability.

* Fresh air and exercise: Languishing in bed may seem to be the easier alternative, but in reality a brisk walk is a better bet.

THE HAIR OF THE DOG

'I Pray thee let me and my fellow have
A hair of the dog that bit us last night.'
Proverbs, John Heywood

This expression originated with the Romans who believed that if you were bitten by a dog you should eat its singed hair (or an infusion of the hair) to prevent the bite from becoming septic. A fanciful idea, but as vaccines have since proved, not so widely far off the mark.

The Prairie Oyster

The night before I had been present at a rather cheery little supper, and I was feeling pretty rocky....

'I was sent by the agency sir,' he said, 'I was given to understand that you required a valet'....

He had a grave, sympathetic face, as if he, too, knew what it was to sup with the lads.

'Excuse me sir,' he said gently.

Then he seemed to flicker and wasn't there any longer. I heard him moving about in the kitchen, and presently he came back with a glass on a tray.

'If you would drink this, sir,' he said, with a kind of bedside manner, rather like the royal doctor shooting the bracer into the sick prince. 'It is a little preparation of my own invention. It is the Worcester Sauce that gives it its colour. The raw egg makes it nutritious. The red pepper gives it its bite. Gentlemen have told me they have found it extremely invigorating after a late evening.'

I would have clutched at anything that looked like a lifeline that morning. I swallowed the stuff. For a moment I felt as if somebody had touched off a bomb inside the old bean and was strolling down my throat with a lighted torch, and then everything seemed suddenly to get all right. The sun shone in through the window; birds twittered in the tree-tops and, generally speaking, hope dawned once more.

'You're engaged!' I said as soon as I could say anything.

Carry On Jeeves, P G Wodehouse

Jeeves' claim to being the inventor of the Prairie Oyster is one of his little exaggerations, but P G Wodehouse may have possibly come across it in the USA.

It is said in the more authoritative version that out on a hunting party in the Texan prairies, one member of the group became ill and developed a craving for oysters—clearly an impossibility hundreds of miles from the sea. With ingenuity, one of his friends broke some hen's eggs carefully into a wine glass, seasoned them, added some vinegar and gave them to the invalid, who duly recovered—hence the name prairie oyster. Whether the gentleman concerned was seriously ill or merely suffering from a severe hangover, history does not relate, but this is the 'connoisseur's cure' and those who are brave enough to try it say it has no equal.

Recipes vary. Some use only the egg yolk, while others omit the Worcestershire sauce and use lemon juice.

1 fresh egg	a dash of cayenne pepper
10 ml/2 tsp Worcestershire sauce	freshly milled black pepper
15 ml/1 tsp vinegar	
a pinch of salt	

Break the egg into a wine glass. Pour over the Worcestershire sauce and vinegar and season with salt, cayenne and black pepper. Close your eyes and drink!

'A drunken night makes a cloudy morning.'
Essays, Sir William Cornwallis, 1601

BLOODY MARY

A good restorative after a heavy night; the amount of vodka varies according to how much is felt to be necessary! Some recipes also contain celery salt, egg whites and sherry—and are almost a complete meal in themselves.

Developed initially at Harry's New York Bar in Paris, where it was known as 'Bucket of Blood' (presumably a reference to the French Revolution), when this drink became popular in New York in the 1940s it was given a rather more genteel name. Mary Tudor, Queen Elizabeth I's half-sister, had universally been known as Bloody Mary.

60 ml/2 fl oz vodka	a dash of Tabasco
120 ml/4 fl oz tomato juice	salt and freshly milled black pepper
7½ ml/¼ fl oz lemon juice	
2.5 ml/½ tsp Worcestershire sauce	

Put all the ingredients into a mixing glass with ice. Stir well, then strain into a tall or ballon glass. Decorate with a slice of lemon and serve.

> 'Drink today and drown all sorrow:
> You shall perhaps not do it tomorrow
> Best while you have it, use your breath;
> There is no drinking after death.'
> *The Bloody Brother*, John Fletcher

THE RITZ REVIVER

A concoction which is gently stirred, not shaken, lest the noise exacerbates the headache. It is not an instantaneous cure—give it half an hour!

15 ml/½ fl oz Cognac	a dash of Angostura bitters
15 ml/½ fl oz Fernet Branca	chilled Champagne
30 ml/1 fl oz fresh orange juice	

Mix the Cognac, Fernet Branca, orange juice and Angostura bitters in a chilled Champagne flute or tulip glass. Top up with Champagne. Sit down quietly and drink.

DEVILLED KIDNEYS

The art of 'devilling' meat and fish, i.e. serving it in a hot, sharp sauce, was originated by the Georgians who had both 'wet' and 'dry' devils. In his introduction to devil sauces in the *Cook's Oracle* published in 1817, Dr Kitchiner clearly considers them to be highly appropriate for the slightly inebriated for he wrote 'Every man must have experienced that when he has got deep into his third bottle...his stomach is seized with a certain craving which seems to demand a stimulant. The provocatives used on such an occasion an ungrateful world has combined to term devils'.

The Victorians took devilling one stage further and ate 'devilled' foods for breakfast, clearly feeling that such dishes might alleviate some of the pain caused by the previous night's revelry.

METRIC/IMPERIAL	•	CUP MEASURES
450 g/1 lb lamb's kidneys		1 lb lamb's kidneys
45 g/1½ oz plain flour		3 tbsp all-purpose flour
50 g/2 oz butter		4 tbsp/½ stick butter
1 large onion, peeled and chopped		1 large onion, peeled and chopped
150 ml/¼ pint beef stock		⅝ cup beef bouillon
10 ml/2 tsp made English mustard		2 tsp made English mustard
15 ml/1 tbsp Worcestershire sauce		1 tbsp Worcestershire sauce
3 anchovy fillets, finely chopped		3 anchovy fillets, finely chopped
freshly milled black pepper		freshly milled black pepper
salt (if necessary)		salt (if necessary)
To garnish:		*To garnish:*
30 ml/2 tbsp chopped parsley		2 tbsp chopped parsley

Serves 4

'Let us have wine, women, mirth and laughter
Sermons and soda water the day after.'
Lord Byron, 1788–1824

Cut the kidneys into 1.25 cm/½ inch pieces, discarding the cores. Toss in the flour. Melt the butter in a pan, add the onion and fry gently for 5 minutes. Increase the heat slightly, add the kidneys and cook for 5 minutes, stirring frequently. Pour in the beef stock, blended with the mustard and Worcestershire sauce and bring to the boil, stirring all the time. Reduce the heat, stir in the anchovies and simmer gently for a further 10 minutes, stirring from time to time. Taste and adjust the seasoning, adding salt if necessary.

Turn into a heated serving dish, sprinkle with the chopped parsley and serve with hot toast.

Index